To

Miss Breanna Champanon

From

Deaconess Shirley Bryant - Harper

Little Book

DEVOTIONS
31 DAILY DEVOTIONALS

Sharing

Little Book

DEVOTIONS

Sharing

The quoted ideas expressed in this book (but not scripture verses) are not, in all cases, exact quotations, as some have been edited for clarity and brevity. In all cases, the author has attempted to maintain the speaker's original intent. In some cases, quoted material for this book was obtained from secondary sources, primarily print media. While every effort was made to ensure the accuracy of these sources, the accuracy cannot be guaranteed. For additions, deletions, corrections or clarifications in future editions of this text, please write BRIGHTON BOOKS.

The Holy Bible, King James Version

The Holy Bible, New King James Version (NKJV) Copyright © 1982 by Thomas Nelson, Inc. Used by permission.

New Century Version®. (NCV) Copyright © 1987, 1988, 1991 by Word Publishing, a division of Thomas Nelson, Inc. All rights reserved. Used by permission.

International Children's Bible®, New Century Version®. (ICB) Copyright © 1986, 1988, 1999 by Tommy Nelson™, a division of Thomas Nelson, Inc. All rights reserved. Used by permission.

The Holman Christian Standard Bible™ (HCSB) Copyright © 1999, 2000, 2001 by Holman Bible Publishers. Used by permission.

The prayers and essays in this book are written by Criswell Freeman; used with permission.

Compiled and Edited: Mary Susan Freeman
Cover Design: Kim Russell, Wahoo Designs
Page Layout: Bart Dawson

ISBN 1-58334-223-0
                    Printed in the United States of America

For All of God's Children

Table of Contents

A Message to Parents

Congratulations on picking up this book—it proves that you're vitally interested in the spiritual and intellectual development of your child.

This text is intended to be read by Christian parents to their young children. The book contains 31 brief chapters, one for each day of the month. Each chapter is composed of a Bible verse, a brief story, helpful hints for kids and for parents, and a prayer. Every chapter examines some aspect of an important Biblical theme: sharing.

For the next 31 days, try this experiment: read one chapter each night to your child, and then spend a few more moments talking about the chapter's meaning. By the end of the month, you will have had 31 different opportunities to share God's wisdom with your son or daughter, and that's a very good thing.

You know how God's love has transformed your own life. Now it's your turn to share that Good News with the boy or girl whom He has entrusted to your care. Happy reading! And may God continue to bless you and yours, now and forever.

Sharing

1

Sharing Is God's Way

If you have two shirts, share with the person who does not have one. If you have food, share that too.

✿ ✿ ✿

Luke 3:11 ICB

You've heard it plenty of times from your parents and teachers: share your things. But it's important to realize that sharing isn't just something that grown-ups want you to do. It's something that God wants you to do too.

The word *possessions* is another way of describing the stuff that belongs to you: your clothes, your toys, your books, and things like these are "your possessions."

Jesus says that you should learn how to share your possessions without feeling bad about it. Sometimes, of course, it's very hard to share and very easy to be stingy. But God wants you to share—and to keep sharing! Since that's what God wants, it's what you should want, too.

What does the Bible say about sharing our possessions? The Bible answers this question very clearly: when other people need our help, we should gladly share the things we have.

WOW

How generous you are does not depend on how much you give, but how much you have left.

Anonymous

Toy referees of the world, unite: It's almost Biblical: when two or more small children are gathered together, they are bound to fuss over toys. Use these disagreements as opportunities to preach the gospel of sharing (even if your sermon falls upon inattentive little ears!).

Dear Lord,
I know there is no happiness
in keeping Your blessings for
myself. Today, I will share
my blessings with my family,
with my friends, and people
who need my help.

Amen

The Golden Rule

2

Do to others what you want them to do to you.

§ § §

Matthew 7:12 NCV

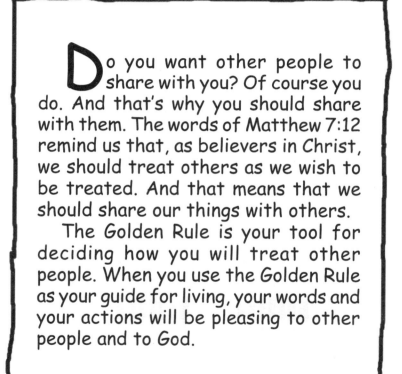

Do you want other people to share with you? Of course you do. And that's why you should share with them. The words of Matthew 7:12 remind us that, as believers in Christ, we should treat others as we wish to be treated. And that means that we should share our things with others.

The Golden Rule is your tool for deciding how you will treat other people. When you use the Golden Rule as your guide for living, your words and your actions will be pleasing to other people and to God.

How would you feel if you were that person? When you're trying to decide how to treat another person, ask yourself this question: "How would I feel if somebody treated me that way?" Then, treat the other person the way that you would want to be treated.

WOW
The Golden Rule starts at home,
but it should never stop there.

Marie T. Freeman

The Golden Rule in Action! When you live according to the principle of the Golden Rule, your children will notice, and the results will be as good as gold . . . make that better than gold!

Dear Lord,
help me always to do my very
best to treat others as I wish
to be treated. The Golden Rule
is Your rule, Father;
let me also make it mine.

Amen

When Sharing Is Hard

3

Remember the words of Jesus. He said,
"It is more blessed to give
than to receive."

§ § §

Acts 20:35 ICB

Jesus said, "It is more blessed to give than to receive." That means that we should be generous with other people—but sometimes we don't feel much like sharing. Instead of sharing the things that we have, we want to keep them all to ourselves. That's when we must remember that God doesn't want selfishness to rule our hearts; He wants us to be generous.

Are you lucky enough to have nice things? If so, God's instructions are clear: you must share your blessings with others. And that's exactly the way it should be. After all, think how generous God has been with you.

Kindness every day: Kindness should be part of our lives every day, not just on the days when we feel good. Don't try to be kind some of the time, and don't try to be kind to some of the people you know. Instead, try to be kind all of the time, and try to be kind to all the people you know. Remember, the Golden Rule starts with you!

WOW
When you worry about what you don't have, you won't be able to enjoy what you do have.
Charles Swindoll

Parental demonstrations on the art of sharing: Your children will learn how to treat others by watching you (not by listening to you!). Your acts of kindness and generosity will speak far louder than words.

Dear Lord,
it's easy to share with some
people and difficult to share
with others. Let me be kind to
all people so that I might follow
in the footsteps of Your Son.

Amen

Kindness 4 Counts

Kind people do themselves a favor,
but cruel people bring trouble
on themselves.

֍ ֍ ֍

Proverbs 11:17 NCV

King Solomon was the man who wrote most of the Book of Proverbs; in it, he gave us lots of helpful advice. Solomon warned that unkind behavior leads only to trouble, but kindness is its own reward.

The next time you're tempted to say or do something unkind, remember Solomon. He was one of the wisest men who ever lived, and he knew that it's always better to be kind. And now, you know it, too.

Kid Tip

You can't just talk about it: In order to be a kind person, you must do kind things. Thinking about them isn't enough. So get busy! The day to start being a more generous person is today!

WOW
If we have the true love of God in our hearts, we will show it in our lives.
D. L. Moody

Respect for all people: Children may seek to find humor in the misfortunes of others; children may, on occasion, exhibit cruelty toward other children. Be watchful for such behaviors and correct them with enthusiasm and vigor.

Dear Lord,
help me to be a kind and
generous person. The Bible
tells me to share my things.
I won't wait to share them;
I will share them now.

Amen

5
Helping People Who Need It

A person who gives to others will get richer. Whoever helps others will himself be helped.

🌀 🌀 🌀

Proverbs 11:25 ICB

Lots of people in the world aren't as fortunate as you are. Some of these folks live in faraway places, and that makes it harder to help them. But other people who need your help are living very near you.

Ask your parents to help you find ways to do something nice for folks who need it. And don't forget that everybody needs love, kindness, and respect, so you should always be ready to share those things, too.

Where can you share? Look around. Soon, you'll have a chance to share a helping hand or a kind word. So keep your eyes open for friends who need your help, whether at home, at church, or at school.

WOW
We hurt people by being too busy,
too busy to notice their needs.
Billy Graham

Parent Tip

Preach, teach, and reach . . . out!: When it comes to teaching our children about helping others, our sermons are not as important as our service. Charity should start at home—with parents—and work its way down the family tree from there.

Dear Lord,
let me help others in every way
that I can. Jesus served others;
I can too. Today, I will share
my possessions and my prayers.
And, I will share kind words
with my family and my friends.

Amen

Sharing with Family

The first thing they need to learn is to do their duty to their own family. When they do this, they will be repaying their parents or grandparents. That pleases God.

꿍 꿍 꿍

1 Timothy 5:4 ICB

A good place to start sharing is at home—but it isn't always an easy place to start. Sometimes, especially when we're tired or mad, we don't treat our family members as nicely as we should. And that's too bad!

Do you have brothers and sisters? Or cousins? If so, you're lucky.

Sharing your things—without whining or complaining—is a wonderful way to show your family that you love them. So the next time a brother or sister or cousin asks to borrow something, say "yes" without getting mad. It's a great way to say, "I love you."

KiD TiP

Since you love your family . . . let them know it by the things you say and the things you do. And, never take your family members for granted; they deserve your very best treatment!

WOW

The first essential for a happy home
is love.

Billy Graham

Parent Tip

As children grow older, give them age-appropriate responsibilities: Household chores can be wonderful teaching tools. Employ them.

Dear Lord,
You have given me a family
that cares for me and loves me.
Thank You. I will let my
family know that I love them
by the things that I say and do.
You know that I love my family,
Lord. Now it's my turn
to show them!

Amen

7

The Things You Don't Need

Those who trust in riches will be ruined.
But a good person will be as healthy
as a green leaf.

৯ ৯ ৯

Proverbs 11:28 ɪᴄʙ

Do you have more toys than you can play with? Do you have clothes that you no longer like to wear? If so, it's time to start thinking about who could use them.

Talk to your parents about ways to share the things you aren't using. Remember this: somebody out there would gladly use these things; in fact, somebody out there needs these things. And it's up to you and your parents to find that somebody—and share.

Finding loving homes for clothes and toys: Your parents can help you find younger children who need the clothes and toys that you've outgrown.

WOW
When we put people before possessions in our hearts, we are sowing seeds of enduring satisfaction.

Beverly LaHaye

A system of family values that is built upon the Rock: It's up to you to insure that your family's value system is built upon the Rock that cannot be moved. As a parent, you must help your children understand that obeying God's Word is a priority that never comes "next."

Dear Lord,
help me make Your world
a better place. I can't fix all
the world's troubles, but I can
make things better here at
home. Help me remember the
importance of sharing the things
that I have and the importance
of sharing the love that
I feel in my heart.

Amen

8 Sharing with Friends

A friend loves you all the time,
and a brother helps in time of trouble.

🆂 🆂 🆂

Proverbs 17:17 NCV

How can you be a good friend? One way is by sharing. And here are some of the things you can share: smiles, kind words, pats on the back, your toys, school supplies, books, and, of course, your prayers.

Would you like to make your friends happy? And would you like to make yourself happy at the same time? Here's how: treat your friends like you want to be treated. That means obeying the Golden Rule, which, of course, means sharing. In fact, the more you share, the better friend you'll be.

Want to make friends? Pay attention! The more interested you are in them, the more interested they will become in you!

WOW

The best times in life are made
a thousand times better when shared
with a dear friend.

Luci Swindoll

Before your child's friends come over for a visit, remind your child that he or she is the host, and that sharing with guests is an important way to demonstrate hospitality.

Dear Lord,
thank You for my friends.
Let me be a trustworthy friend
to others, and let my love
for You be reflected in
my genuine love for them.

Amen

What the Bible Says

9

Your word is like a lamp for my feet
and a light for my way.

֍ ֍ ֍

Psalm 119:105 ICB

What book contains everything that God has to say about sharing? The Bible, of course. If you read the Bible every day, you'll soon be convinced that sharing is very important to God. And, since sharing is important to God, it should be important to you, too.

The Bible is the most important book you'll ever own. It's God's Holy Word. Read it every day, and follow its instructions. If you do, you'll be safe now and forever.

KiD TiP

Read the Bible? Every day!: try to read your Bible with your parents every day. If they forget, remind them!

WOW

Some read the Bible to learn, and some read the Bible to hear from heaven.

Andrew Murray

Parent Tip

It's up to us: Our children will learn about Jesus at church and, in some cases, at school. But, the ultimate responsibility for religious teachings should never be delegated to institutions outside the home. As parents, we must teach our children about the love and grace of Jesus Christ by our words and by our actions.

Dear Lord,
the Bible is Your gift to me.
Let me use it, let me trust it,
and let me obey it, today
and every day that I live.

Amen

10
Sharing
Cheerfully

God loves the person who gives happily.

🌀 🌀 🌀

2 Corinthians 9:7 ICB

How many times have you heard someone say, "Don't touch that; it's mine!" If you're like most of us, you've heard those words many times and you may have even said them yourself.

The Bible tells us that it's better for us to share things than it is to keep them all to ourselves. And the Bible also tells us that when we share, it's best to do so cheerfully. So today and every day, let's share. It's the best way because it's God's way.

When am I old enough to start giving?
If you're old enough to understand these words, you're old enough to start giving to your church and to those who are less fortunate than you. If you're not sure about the best way to do it, ask your parents!

WOW
Selfishness is as far from Christianity
as darkness is from light.
C. H. Spurgeon

Cheerfulness is contagious: Remember that a cheerful family starts with cheerful parents.

Dear Lord,
make me a generous and
cheerful Christian. Let me be
kind to those who need my
encouragement, and let me share
with those who need my help,
today and every day.

Amen

It Comes from the Heart

Every way of a man is right in his
own eyes, but the LORD weighs the hearts.

🌀 🌀 🌀

Proverbs 21:2 NKJV

Other people see you from the outside. God sees you from the inside—God sees your heart.

Kindness comes from the heart. So does sharing. So if you want to show your family and your friends that your heart is filled with kindness and love, one way to do it is by sharing. But don't worry about trying to show God what kind of person you are. He already knows your heart, and He loves you more than you can imagine.

KiD TiP

Talk about your feelings: If something is bothering you, tell your parents. Don't be afraid to talk about your feelings. Your mom and dad love you, and they can help you. So whatever "it" is, talk about it . . . with your parents!

WOW

It is the thoughts and intents of
the heart that shape a person's life.

John Eldredge

Parent Tip

Be expressive: Make certain that at your house, love is expressed and demonstrated many times each day. Little acts of consideration and kindness can make a big difference in the way that your child views the world.

Dear Lord,
thank You for loving me.
I will return Your love
by sharing it . . .
today and every day.

Amen

12

You're an Example

In every way be an example of doing good deeds.

෯ ෯ ෯

Titus 2:7 NCV

What kind of example are you? Are you the kind of person who shows other people what it means to share? Hopefully you are that kind of person!!!

Whether you realize it or not, you're an example to your friends and family members. So today, be a good example for others to follow. Because God needs people (like you) who are willing to behave themselves as God intends. And that's exactly the kind of example you should always try to be.

Your friends are watching: Be the kind of example that God wants you to be: a good example.

WOW
Our walk counts far more
than our talk, always!
George Mueller

Live according to the principles you teach: The sermons you live are far more important than the sermons you preach.

Dear Lord,
make me a good example to
my family and friends.
Let the things that I say and
do show everybody what it
means to be a good person and
a good Christian.

Amen

13
The Best Time to Share

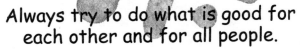

Always try to do what is good for
each other and for all people.

۶ ۶ ۶

1 Thessalonians 5:15 ICB

When is the best time to share? Whenever you can—and that means right now, if possible. When you start thinking about the things you can share, you probably think mostly about things that belong to you (like toys or clothes), but there are many more things you can share (like love, kindness, encouragement, and prayers). That means you have the opportunity to share something with somebody almost anytime you want. And that's exactly what God wants you to do—so start sharing now and don't ever stop.

How about sharing a hug right now? The person who's reading you this book deserves one!

WOW
Life is a glorious opportunity.
Billy Graham

The importance of "now": As a parent, you know that procrastination is an easy habit to acquire and a difficult habit to break. When the time is right, help your child learn the value of self-discipline and the importance of doing first things first.

Dear Lord,
there are so many things that
I can share. Help me never to
forget the importance of
sharing my possessions,
my prayers, and my love with
family members and friends.

Amen

How They Know You're a Christian

14

Beloved, if God so loved us,
we also ought to love one another.

§ § §

1 John 4:11 NKJV

How do people know that you're a Christian? Well, you can tell them, of course. And make no mistake about it: talking about your faith in God is a very good thing to do. But telling people about Jesus isn't enough. You should also show people how a Christian (like you) should behave.

God wants you to be loving and giving. That way, when another person sees how you behave, that person will know what it means to be a good Christian . . . a good Christian like you!

KID TIP

Christians are . . . kind and respectful: As a Christian, you must make sure that you show proper respect for everyone, even if that person happens to be different from you. It's easy to make fun of people who seem different . . . but it's wrong.

WOW
A person ought to live so that everybody knows he is a Christian.

D. L. Moody

Be expressive: Make certain that your own faith in God is expressed and demonstrated many times each day. Frequent expressions of worship and praise will make a big difference in the life of your child.

Dear Lord,
help me to make Your world
a better place. I can't fix all
the world's troubles, but I can
help make things better with
kind words, good deeds, and
sincere prayers. Let my
actions and my prayers be
pleasing to You, Lord,
now and forever.

Amen

It's Tempting to Be Selfish

15

When you do things, do not let selfishness
or pride be your guide. Be humble
and give more honor to others
than to yourselves.

〰 〰 〰

Philippians 2:3 ICB

It's tempting to be selfish, but it's wrong. It's tempting to want to keep everything for yourself, but it's better to share. It's tempting to say, "No, that's MINE!" but it's better to say, "I'll share it with you."

Are you sometimes tempted to be a little stingy? Are you sometimes tempted to say, "No, I don't want to share that!"—and then do you feel a little sorry that you said it? If that describes you, don't worry: everybody is tempted to be a little bit selfish. Your job is to remember this: even when it's tempting to be selfish, you should try very hard not to be. Because when you're generous, not selfish, you'll make your parents proud and you'll make your Father in heaven proud, too.

Tempted to get into an argument? Walk away. The best fights are those that never happen.

WOW
Selfishness is as far from Christianity as darkness is from light.

C. H. Spurgeon

When it comes to courteous behavior, you're the most important role model: so pay careful attention to the way that you treat other people, especially those who are not in a position to help you. For further instructions, read Matthew 25:40.

Dear Lord,
Your Son Jesus was never
selfish. Let me follow in
His footsteps by sharing
with those who need my help.

Amen

16
Learning to Share

Assuredly, I say to you, inasmuch
as you did it to one of the least of these
My brethren, you did it to Me.

§ § §

Matthew 25:40 NKJV

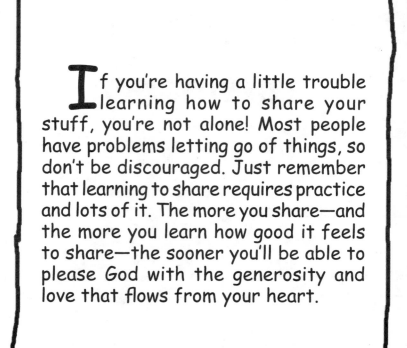

If you're having a little trouble learning how to share your stuff, you're not alone! Most people have problems letting go of things, so don't be discouraged. Just remember that learning to share requires practice and lots of it. The more you share—and the more you learn how good it feels to share—the sooner you'll be able to please God with the generosity and love that flows from your heart.

Practice, practice, practice: Want to get good at sharing? Start by sharing little things, and work your way up from there.

WOW
Begin to know Christ now, and finish never.
Oswald Chambers

Sharing every day . . . Each day offers countless opportunities to share. Seize these opportunities. When you do, you'll help your child understand that sharing should be woven into the fabric of everyday events.

Dear Lord,
help me to learn the importance
of sharing. The Bible teaches
me to share, and so do my
parents. Now, it's up to me to
learn how to share the things
that I have—and it's up to me to
share kind words and good deeds
with my family and friends.

Amen

17

It Makes You a Better Person

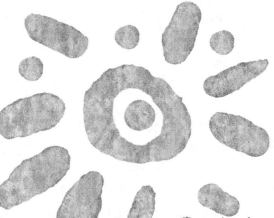

Happy is the person who thinks
about the poor.

ى ى ى

Psalm 41:1 NCV

It's a fact: sharing makes you a better person. Why? Because when you share, you're doing several things: first, you're obeying God; you're making your corner of the world a better place; and you're learning exactly what it feels like to be a generous, loving person.

When you share, you have the fun of knowing that your good deeds are making other people happy. When you share, you're learning how to become a better person. When you share, you're making things better for other people and for yourself. So do the right thing: share!

Would you like to be a little happier? The Bible says that if you become a more generous person, you'll become a happier person, too.

WOW
Happiness is obedience to God.
C. H. Spurgeon

Cheerful generosity is contagious: Kids catch it from their parents.

Dear Lord,
I can't really enjoy my blessings
until I share them. Let me learn
to be a generous person, and
let me say "thanks" to You by
sharing some of the gifts that
You have already given me.

Amen

18

Learning from the Master

Mary was sitting at Jesus' feet
and listening to him teach.

⚈ ⚈ ⚈

Luke 10:39 ICB

Who was the greatest teacher in the history of the world? Jesus was . . and He still is! Jesus teaches us how to live, how to behave, and how to worship. Now, it's up to each of us, as Christians, to learn the important lessons that Jesus can teach.

Someday soon, you will have learned everything that Jesus has to teach you, right? WRONG!!!! Jesus will keep teaching you important lessons throughout your life. And that's good, because all of us, kids and grown-ups alike, have lots to learn . . . especially from the Master . . . and the Master, of course, is Jesus.

Learning about Jesus: Start learning about Jesus, and keep learning about Him as long as you live. His story never grows old, and His teachings never fail.

WOW

Nobody ever outgrows Scripture;
the book widens and deepens
with our years.

C. H. Spurgeon

Parent Tip

We've still got lots to learn, too! When it comes to studying the Bible, none of us ever "graduate" —when it comes to studying the Bible, school is always in session. Bible study should be a lifelong endeavor; make it your lifelong endeavor.

PRAY TIME

Dear Lord,
You are my Teacher.
Help me to learn from You.
And then, let me show others
what it means to be a kind,
generous, loving Christian.

Amen

19

Solomon Says

Here is my final advice:
Honor God and obey his commands.

〰 〰 〰

Ecclesiastes 12:13 ICB

Solomon wasn't just a king. He was also a very wise man and a very good writer. He even wrote several books in the Bible! So when He finally put down His pen, what was this wise man's final advice? It's simple: Solomon said, "Honor God and obey His commandments."

The next time you have an important choice to make, ask yourself this: "Am I honoring God and obeying Him? And am I doing what God wants me to do?" If you can answer those questions with a great big "YES", then go ahead. But if you're uncertain if the choice you are about to make is the right one, slow down. Why? Because that's what Solomon says . . . and that's what God says, too!

Simon says? Solomon says! Have you ever played the game Simon Says? When you play it, you're not supposed to move until the leader calls out, "Simon Says!" Wise King Solomon had many rules for living. You should get to know those rules—especially the ones found in the Book of Proverbs. Then, you can be guided by the things that Solomon says!

WOW
God's mark is on everything
that obeys Him.
Martin Luther

Get to know the Book of Proverbs, and help your child get to know it, too (a children's translation of the Bible can help!).

Dear Lord,
when I play by Your rules,
You give me wonderful rewards.
I will read the Bible, Lord,
so I can learn Your rules—
and I will obey Your rules,
today and always.

Amen

It's a Habit

Do not be fooled:
"Bad friends will ruin good habits."

§ § §

1 Corinthians 15:33 NCV

Our lives are made up of lots and lots of habits. These habits help determine the kind of people we become. If we choose habits that are good, we are happier and healthier. If we choose habits that are bad, then it's too bad for us!

Sharing, like so many other things, is a habit. And it's a habit that is right for you.

Do you want to grow up to become the kind of person that God intends for you to be? Then get into the habit of sharing the gifts that your Heavenly Father has given you. You'll be glad you did . . . and so will God!

Choose your habits carefully: Habits are easier to make than they are to break, so be careful!

WOW

Prayer is a habit. Worship is a habit. Kindness is a habit. And if you want to please God, you'd better make sure that these habits are your habits.

Marie T. Freeman

The importance of having healthy habits: The old saying is familiar and true: "First you make your habits; then your habits make you." So it's always a good time to ask this question: "What kind of person are my habits making me?"

Dear Lord,
help me form good habits.
And let me make a habit of
sharing the things that
I own and the love that
I feel in my heart.

Amen

Sharing with Your Church

For we are God's fellow workers;
you are God's field, you are God's building.

⑤ ⑤ ⑤

1 Corinthians 3:9 NKJV

When the offering plate passes by, are you old enough to drop anything in it? If you are, congratulations! But if you're not quite old enough to give money to the church, don't worry—there are still lots of things you can share!

Even when you don't have money to share, you still have much to give to your church. What are some things you can share? Well, you can share your smile, your happiness, your laughter, your energy, your cooperation, your prayers, your obedience, your example, and your love.

So don't worry about giving to the church: even if you don't have lots of money, there are still plenty of ways you can give. And the best time to start giving is NOW!

Got money? Share it! Have you ever earned money for doing things around the house? Or have you ever received money as a gift? If so, ask your parents to help you decide on the best way to share some of it.

WOW
Joyful living means joyful giving.
E. Stanley Jones

Teaching generosity: It's never too early to emphasize the importance of giving. From the time that a child is old enough to drop a penny into the offering plate, we, as parents, should stress the obligation that we all have to share the blessings that God has shared with us.

Dear Lord,
thank You for my church.
When I am at church, I will be
generous, kind, well behaved,
and respectful. And when
I am not at church,
I will act the same way.

Amen

Too Young to Share?

You are young, but do not let anyone
treat you as if you were not important.

§ § §

1 Timothy 4:12 ICB

How old should you be before you should start learning how to share your stuff? If you're old enough to understand these words (and you are!), then you're plenty old enough to learn how to become a person who cooperates and shares.

Have you noticed that small babies aren't very good at sharing? No wonder! They're too young to know better—but you're not. So do what you know is right: share!

With more birthdays comes better behavior: As you grow up, you'll keep learning better ways to behave yourself. The more candles on your birthday cake, the better you'll be expected to behave—and the easier it will become to behave yourself.

WOW

The maturity of a Christian cannot be reached in a moment. All of us are growing up in Christ.

Hannah Whitall Smith

Age level *and* maturity level matter: Be sure that the expectations you hold for your child are appropriate for his or her stage of development. As the old saying goes: "kids will be kids." And as a responsible parent, you should let your kid be one, too.

Dear Lord,
while I am growing up,
I still have so many things
to learn. Let me remember that
the most important lessons
are the ones that I learn
every day from my parents
and from You.

Amen

23

When Others Don't Share

I tell you, love your enemies.
Pray for those who hurt you.
If you do this, you will be true sons of
your Father in heaven.

֍ ֍ ֍

Matthew 6:44-45 ICB

Face it: sometimes people aren't nice. And when other people don't share, you may be tempted to strike out in anger. Don't do it! Instead, remember that God corrects other people's behaviors in His own way, and He probably doesn't need your help. And remember that God has commanded you to forgive other people, just as you seek forgiveness from others when you misbehave. So, when other people aren't nice, forgive them as quickly as you can. And leave the rest up to God.

Count to ten . . . and keep counting: If you're mad at someone, don't say the first thing that comes to your mind and don't strike out in anger. Instead, catch your breath and start counting until you are once again in control of your temper. If you get to a million and you're still counting, go to bed! You'll feel better in the morning.

WOW
Nothing is really ours until we share it.

C. S. Lewis

Wise role models are a good thing to have: If you can control your anger, you'll help your children see the wisdom in controlling theirs.

Dear Lord,
when I become angry,
help me to remember that
You offer me peace. Let me turn
to You for wisdom, for patience,
and for the peace that
only You can give.

Amen

24

Helping Others Is Fun

Happy is the person who . . .
loves what the LORD commands.

🌀 🌀 🌀

Psalm 112:1 ICB

Helping other people can be fun! When you help others, you feel better about yourself. And, you know that God approves of what you're doing.

When you learn how to cooperate with your family and friends, you'll soon discover that it's more fun when everybody works together. And one way that you can all work together is by sharing.

So do yourself a favor: learn better ways to share and to cooperate. It's the right thing to do, and, besides, it's more fun.

Do you need a little cheering up? Cheer up somebody else. When you brighten some-body else's day, you brighten up your own day, too.

WOW

Do all the good you can. In all the ways
you can. In all the places you can.
At all the times you can. To all the people
you can. As long as you can.

John Wesley

Cheerfulness is contagious: Remember that a cheerful family starts with cheerful parents.

Dear Lord,
Your love is so wonderful that
I can't really imagine it,
but I can share it . . .
and I will . . .
today and every day.

Amen

The World Needs You

You are the light that gives light to the world . . . Live so that they will see the good things you do. Live so that they will praise your Father in heaven.

৩ ৩ ৩

Matthew 5:14,16 ICB

The Bible says that you are "the light that gives light to the world." The Bible also says that you should live in a way that lets other people understand what it means to be a good person. And of course, learning to share is an important part of being a good person.

What kind of "light" have you been giving off? Hopefully, you have been a good example for everybody to see. Why? Because the world needs all the light it can get, and that includes your light, too!

Let your light shine by being respectful: Everybody is important to God. And you should treat every person with courtesy, dignity, and respect.

WOW
It is a great deal better to live
a holy life than to talk about it.
Lighthouses do not ring bells,
they just shine.

D. L Moody

Living your life and shining your light . . . on your children: As a parent, the most important light you shine is the light that your own life shines on the lives of your children. May your light shine brightly, righteously, obediently, and eternally!

Dear Lord,
let my light shine brightly for
You. Let me be a good example
for all to see, and let me share
love and kindness with my family
and friends, today and every day.

Amen

26 Too Much Stuff

Then Jesus said to them, "Be careful
and guard against all kinds of greed.
A man's life is not measured by
the many things he owns."

৯ ৯ ৯

Luke 12:15 ɪᴄʙ

Are you one of those kids who is lucky enough to have a closet filled up with stuff? If so, it's probably time to share some of it.

When your mom or dad says it's time to clean up your closet and give some things away, don't be sad. Instead of whining, think about all the children who could enjoy the things that you don't use very much. And while you're at it, think about what Jesus might tell you to do if He were here. Jesus would tell you to share generously and cheerfully. And that's exactly what you should do!

KiD TiP

Too many toys? Give them away! Are you one of those lucky kids who has more toys than you can play with? If so, remember that not everyone is so lucky. Ask your parents to help you give some of your toys to children who need them more than you do.

WOW

If you want to be truly happy,
you won't find it on a never-ending search
for more stuff.

Bill Hybels

Giving away stuff, holding on to memories: As your child grows into adulthood, some of the most precious possessions from their childhood will be memories. So keep lots of photos, journals, notes from friends and family, and a few treasured keepsakes. As hard as it is to believe, your little angels will grow up sooner than you can imagine. And when they do, one of the greatest gifts you can give them is a box full (and a heart full) of happy memories.

119

PRAY TiME

Dear Lord,
sometimes it's easy to think
only of myself and not of
others. Help me remember that
I should treat other people
in the same way that I would
want to be treated if I were
standing in their shoes. You have
given me many blessings, Lord—
let me share them now.

Amen

27
The Good Samaritan

Then a Samaritan traveling down the road came to where the hurt man was. When he saw the man, he felt very sorry for him. The Samaritan went to him, poured olive oil and wine on his wounds, and bandaged them. Then he put the hurt man on his own donkey and took him to an inn where he cared for him.

෨ ෨ ෨

Luke 10:33-34 NCV

Sometimes we would like to help make the world a happier place, but we're not sure how to do it. Jesus told the story of the "Good Samaritan," a man who helped a fellow traveler when no one else would. We, too, should be good Samaritans when we find people who need our help.

So what can you do to make God's world a better place? You can start by making your own corner of the world a little nicer place to live (by sharing kind words and good deeds). And then, you can take your concerns to God in prayer. Whether you've offered a helping hand or a heartfelt prayer, you've done a lot.

KiD TiP

Does a friend or family member need your help? Then be a Good Samaritan by sharing a helping hand, a friendly word, or a happy smile.

WOW

When somebody needs a helping hand, he doesn't need it tomorrow or the next day. He needs it now, and that's exactly when you should offer to help. Good deeds, if they are really good, happen sooner rather than later.

Marie T. Freeman

Parent Tip

Good Samaritan 101: You're the teacher. Class is in session. Your child is in attendance. Actions speak louder than words. And it's one of the most important courses you will ever teach.

Dear Lord,
when my family or friends need
me, let me behave myself like
the Good Samaritan.
Let me be helpful, generous,
and kind . . . today, tomorrow,
and every day of my life.

Amen

28
Pray about It!

When a believing person prays,
great things happen.

ఌ ఌ ఌ

James 5:16 NCV

If you are upset, pray about it. If you're having trouble sharing, ask God to help you. If there is a person you don't like, pray for a forgiving heart. If there is something you're worried about, ask God to comfort you.

As you pray more and more, you'll discover that God is always near and that He's always ready to hear from you. So don't worry about things; pray about them. God is waiting . . . and listening!

Open-eyed prayers: When you are praying, your eyes don't always have to be closed. Of course it's good to close your eyes and bow your head, but you can also offer a quick prayer to God with your eyes open. That means that you can pray just about anytime you want.

WOW

Some people think God does not like
to be troubled with our constant asking.
But, the way to trouble God is
not to ask Him at all.

D. L. Moody

Don't ever be embarrassed to pray: Are you embarrassed to bow your head in a restaurant? Don't be; it's the people who don't pray in restaurants who should be embarrassed!

Dear Lord,
help me remember
the importance of prayer.
You always hear my prayers, God;
let me always pray them!

Amen

29

You'll Feel Better about Yourself

So prepare your minds for service
and have self-control. All your hope should
be for the gift of grace that will be yours
when Jesus Christ is shown to you.

🎵 🎵 🎵

1 Peter 1:13 NCV

The more you share, the quicker you'll discover this fact: Good things happen to people (like you) who are kind enough to share the blessings that God has given them.

Sharing makes you feel better about yourself. Whether you're at home or at school, remember that the best rewards go to the kids who are kind and generous—not to the people who are unkind or stingy. So do what's right: share. You'll feel lots better about yourself when you do.

Feeling better about yourself by helping other people: When talking to other people, ask yourself this question: "How helpful can I be?" When you help others, you'll be proud of yourself, and God will be, too!

WOW
The way you see yourself and
the world has a whole lot to do
with how happy you are.
Zig Ziglar

Feeling good about yourself: The perfect parent does not exist. So don't be too hard on yourself when you fall short of absolute perfection (or, for that matter, when you fall short of near-perfection). Do your best, and trust God with the rest.

Dear Lord,
help me to slow down and
to think about my behavior.
And then, help me to do
the right thing, so that I can
feel better about myself . . .
and You can, too.

Amen

30
God Knows
Your Heart

I am the LORD, and I can look
into a person's heart.

🌀 🌀 🌀

Jeremiah 17:10 ICB

Even when nobody else is watching, God is. Nothing that we say or do escapes the watchful eye of our Father in heaven.

God understands that we are not perfect, but even though He knows that we make mistakes, He still wants us to live according to His rules, not our own.

The next time that you're tempted to say something that you shouldn't say or to do something that you shouldn't do, remember that you can't keep secrets from God. So don't even try!

Big, bigger, and very big plans. God has very big plans in store for you, so trust Him, and do your best to obey His rules.

WOW

When you extend hospitality to others,
you're not trying to impress people,
you're trying to reflect God to them.

Max Lucado

Make Christ the cornerstone: Every family is built upon something; let the foundation of your family be the love of God and the salvation of Christ.

PRAY TIME

Dear Lord,
You know my heart. And,
You have given me a conscience
that tells me what is right
and what is wrong. I will listen
to that quiet voice so I can do
the right thing today
and every day.

Amen

31

What Jesus Shares with You

For God loved the world in this way: He gave His only Son, so that everyone who believes in Him will not perish but have eternal life.

֍ ֍ ֍

John 3:16 HCSB

Who's the best friend this world has ever had? Jesus, of course! When you invite Him into your heart, Jesus will be your friend, too . . . your friend forever.

Jesus has offered to share the gifts of everlasting life and everlasting love with the world . . . and with you. If you make mistakes, He'll still be your friend. If you behave badly, He'll still love you. If you feel sorry or sad, He can help you feel better.

Jesus wants you to have a happy, healthy life. He wants you to be generous and kind. He wants you to follow His example. And the rest is up to you. You can do it! And with a friend like Jesus, you will.

When in doubt, think about Him. When you have an important decision to make, stop for a minute and think about how Jesus would behave if He were in your shoes.

WOW
Christ's love is like a river
that never stops flowing.
Jonathan Edwards

Jesus loves you, this you know . . . and they should too! Of course you know that Jesus loves you. But it's up to you to make sure that they know that you know. So remind them often.

Dear Lord,
thank You for Your Son. Jesus
loves me and He shares so much
with me. Let me share His love
with others so that through me,
they can understand what
it means to follow Him.

Amen

Bible Verses to Memorize

God loves the person
who gives happily.

🌀 🌀 🌀

2 Corinthians 9:7 ICB

The LORD is my shepherd;
I shall not want. He makes
me to lie down in green
pastures; He leads me
beside the still waters.
He restores my soul.

❈ ❈ ❈

Psalm 23:1-3 NKJV

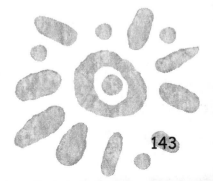

Draw near to God,
and He will draw near
to you.

James 4:8 HCSB

I have come that they
may have life, and that
they may have it
more abundantly.

🕉 🕉 🕉

John 10:10 NKJV

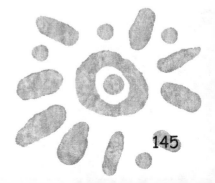

Wisdom begins with respect for the LORD.

Proverbs 9:10 ICB

Now these three remain: faith, hope, and love. But the greatest of these is love.

෨ ෨ ෨

1 Corinthians 13:13 HCSB

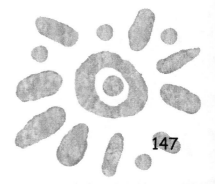

We love Him because
He first loved us.

ৡ ৡ ৡ

1 John 4:19 NKJV

Be still, and know that I am God . . . .

৯ ৯ ৯

Psalm 46:10 KJV

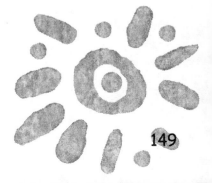

I tell you, love your enemies.
Pray for those who hurt you.
If you do this,
you will be true sons of
your Father in heaven.

☙ ☙ ☙

Matthew 6:44-45 ICB

Jesus said to him, "You shall love the Lord your God with all your heart, with all your soul, and with all your mind. This is the first and great commandment. And the second is like it: 'You shall love your neighbor as yourself."

〆 〆 〆

Matthew 22:37-39 NKJV

Trust the Lord with all your heart. Don't depend on your own understanding. Remember the Lord in everything you do. And he will give you success.

Proverbs 3:5-6 ICB

I am able to do all things through Him who strengthens me.

❋ ❋ ❋

Philippians 4:13 HCSB

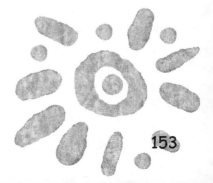

Let not your heart
be troubled;
you believe in God,
believe also in Me.

❋ ❋ ❋

John 14:1 NKJV

This is the day that
the LORD has made.
Let us rejoice
and be glad today!

೫ ೫ ೫

Psalm 118:24 ICB

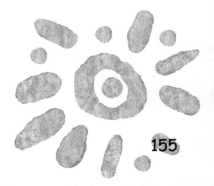

For God so loved the world,
that he gave his only
begotten Son, that
whosoever believeth in
him should not perish,
but have everlasting life.

❈ ❈ ❈

John 3:16 KJV

For the LORD is good;
His mercy is everlasting,
and His truth endures
to all generations.

❄ ❄ ❄

Psalm 100:5 NKJV

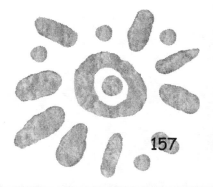